CW00867848

HOW TO MOVE TO DUBAI

Real estate Edition

Giving You An In-Depth Insight On
How To Make The Move

COPYRIGHT © 2023 OFF THE BUX. ALL RIGHTS RESERVED.

NO PART OF THIS EBOOK MAY BE REPRODUCED, STORED IN
A RETRIEVAL SYSTEM, OR TRANSMITTED IN ANY FORM OR BY
ANY MEANS, ELECTRONIC, MECHANICAL, PHOTOCOPYING,
RECORDING, OR OTHERWISE, WITHOUT THE PRIOR WRITTEN

PERMISSION OF OFF THE BUX.

CONTENTS

MY PERSONAL EXPERIENCE

Hi, my name is Elise and I made this e-book for those considering taking the leap and moving to Dubai. I have been here for a year now and I wish there was something like this when I was in the process of moving because, to be honest with you, I had no clue what I was doing. I winged everything and went with the flow which when I think back, was so scary for me at 22 years old. Moving to a new country can be daunting without any knowledge so hopefully, this helps in some way or another to give you an insight into how to make the move, and what the next steps are and support you through your first few weeks in Dubai.

INSTAGRAM @ X_ELISESTAN

WHERE AND HOW TO APPLY

When looking for the right company to join, make sure you do your research.
There are so many different real estate companies here in Dubai that one may appeal more to your needs and way of work.

Here is a list of 10 Real Estate agencies in Dubai to apply for:

Luxfolio Real Estate: @luxfoliorealestate

Fam Properties: @famproperties

Better Homes: @betterhomesuae

Allsopp and Allsopp: @allsoppandallsopp

Haus & Haus: @hausandhaus

D&B Properties: @dandbdubai

McCone Properties: @mcconeproperties

Provident Real Estate: @providentestate

White & Co: @Whiteandcodxb

Elysian: @elysiangroup

I would highly recommend you keep up to date with a few of the agencies that interest you via social media so you can get true insights into the day-to-day life in the office and get a true feel of the different companies.

If you're looking for the extra bit of support through the applying and interview process, then you can also use recruitment agencies such as
GuyLast Recruitment.

They take the pressure off by knowing how and which companies to apply you for and help organise all of your interviews.

I would 100% recommend sitting with your family/friends and discussing your options so they can also give you advice on which companies to apply to. They know you more than you probably think they do and having them there to support you and guide you, can really help you make the best decision.

Keeping your LinkedIn profile up-to-date can also help land you the perfect job. Relocation agents may reach out to you via LinkedIn in relation your interests and skills.

Moreover, it is also a great platform for you to connect with other brokers or recruitment agents.

When applying for these roles, make sure you have a date in mind that you could/want to move by. Giving yourself an exact day ensures that you have a deadline to work towards and that you are serious about moving. Letting the interviewer know also shows them you are ready to commit.

INTERVIEW PROCESS

Specific to real estate job roles, qualifications and previous experience is not completely necessary.

The best piece of advice that I can give you, is just to be yourself. Let your personality come through because grades and experience mean nothing if the interviewer finds you boring.

Do some research on the company that you are applying to. Impress the interviewer with facts about the business or even names of people who you've spoken to in the office.

Be on time!

Make sure, whether the interview is on zoom or in person, you attend the interview a few minutes before the scheduled time to show you are ready and prepared.

It will also allow you time to compose yourself and give you the best chance of having a great interview.

Ask questions!

This is vital for any job interview you attend.

Where do you see the company in 5 years?

What is your favourite part about the company?

What are the benefits of joining company x over company y?

What date can I start?

After the interview, arrange a follow-up with the interviewer so you have a timeframe of when you'll have an answer by.

PREPARING TO MOVE

Depending upon how quickly you want the process to happen, you could have a few months to prepare yourself or if you're anything like me and very impatient, you could have it all done within 3/4 weeks.

However, my biggest piece of advice is to save at least £10,000. Moving without the right amount of money can put a lot of strain and pressure on you, which when being in a commission-only role, can ultimately mean you may not be able to survive if you aren't doing any deals. You should try to give yourself the best head start and chance at making real estate work because it can pay off.

Once you've accepted a job role within a company and finalised your move date, there are some obvious next steps you need to make:

Inform your family/friends.

Hand in your notice at your current job.

Work your notice period. If you have an employment contract or union agreement that states how much notice you should give, abide by it.

Leave some time between leaving your job and your move date to organise finances and other responsibilities.

Settle any debts.

The best advice I can give to anyone looking to move to any new country or place is to join as many Facebook groups as possible. There is so much day-to-day advice and help in these chats and it's also a great way to meet new friends and people who are also in the same boat as you.

The main groups are:

Brits in Dubai

ATB Dubai X The Invite Said Casual (girls only)

You can also join community groups for the area you live in or work in. (Facebook groups will also help in the long run when the time comes you're looking to furnish an apartment).

Even meeting a few girls from these groups in the UK before you move out, can jump-start your Dubai experience and give you that extra support instead of doing it on your own, which can be so daunting.

Make sure you celebrate with family and friends. Enjoy spending the last few weeks with them before you disembark across the world.

I'm sorry to say but this is one of the most stressful parts of moving and make sure you stick to your baggage allowance with the flights you book, you can also bring move over when you visit home.

BOOKING YOUR ACCOMMODATION

Finding accommodation can be the most challenging/stressful part of the whole process, especially if you've never visited Dubai.

The biggest misconception is that you can walk from place to place. Unfortunately, this is not possible so finding the right area to live in, that is:

Close to work.

Close to public transport if needed, is vital.

The best starting point is to find out where the company you will be working for is based, this will you give a rough idea of which surrounding areas may be suitable.

Next, I would recommend setting yourself a budget. Different areas in Dubai can cost more than offers depending upon many factors.

This will help filter your search for areas you can afford.

To rent an apartment for a full year, you will need your Emirates ID and bank account before you sign for a property. So for the first few months, you will most likely rent short term.

This will also help you determine which area you might rent for the long term.
Or, of course staying with friends, which will also help you save money.

You can you the below websites to help find and book your accommodation:

Property Finder - UAE's most used platform to rent a property however you need an emirates ID before renting for one year

Dubizzle - This is good for those who do not want to pay agency commission and want to rent direct from the owner.

Facebook groups - This is the best place to get started as you don't need an Emirates ID. You can usually rent on a month-to-month basis and meet friends along the way whilst your house sharing. There are always spare rooms being offered in different groups and a great way to save money.

FYI- just to give you some inside info:

When looking for a long term rental you will be required to pay in cheques.

This is most probably something you haven't heard of before and its simply just a way of paying your rent.

1 Cheque - payment in full.
2 Cheques - payment for 6 months upfront.
4 Cheques - payments quarterly.

WHAT TO BRING

The main thing is your passport. Also making sure there is plenty of time left on your passport. Dubai is a great location to be able to travel the world and once the job is really clicking, you most definitely will want to take a few holidays and time off to relax.

Bringing a few extra passport photos for your visa and other documents is also advisable.

When packing your bags, remember the weather usually sits at 25-30 degrees in the winter and anything from 30+ in the summer. So coats and warm clothes won't be, however, on the winter nights, it can get slightly chilly so I would still recommend bringing jeans and tracksuits.

There are a few things that I would class as 'essential' that you definitely should consider bulk buying before getting on the plane that will save you some money once you're out here:

Dry shampoo
Makeup Wipes
English Chocolate (Chocolate in the UAE is
different)
Underwear
Medication (Check UAE rules)

You can still get everything you need when you arrive out here, it's just it can be more expensive and at the start, you will want to save as much money as possible.

APPS TO DOWNLOAD

I would recommend downloading these apps a few days before you land or once you land in Dubai because some of them are lifesavers. (Some are just for girls, sorry boys)

Careem - provides taxi service, delivery services and much more. It is the most essential app.

Deliveroo - As I'm sure most are aware already, it is for all food deliveries.

Instashop - This one is the most life-changing app. You can almost get everything delivered on this app to your door within minutes.

Carrefour - is the biggest supermarket in the UAE and you can have a full weeks worth of shopping delivered for a delivery fee of 5AED in 60 minutes.

Kibsons- Kibsons is great for UK expats as most of it is either Tesco or Sainsbury's.

Entertainer - with the Entertainer, you pay a yearly subscription to have access to 100's of offers on food, attractions, hotel stays and much more. Definitely worth the money.

Priverlee - This app will you give you discount or free entry to pool days, spas and discount on food.

TSS- (The Secret Society) free meals and days out for girls.

Alist- Very similar to TSS, it gives you different options to TSS.

Safe driver - A driver to drive you home after a drink.

Cafu - Petrol/ Diesel delivery service to your home

Waze - One of the easiest ways to get directions and you don't need data

HOW TO GET A MOBILE SIM

Once you arrive in Dubai at the airport, they will usually hand you a DU tourist sim.

This is great to use for a short period before you get yourself set up. My advice would be to go as soon as possible to a mall and set up your phone sim sooner rather than later.

There are three major providers in the UAE, DU, Virgin Mobile and Etisalat.

Du and Etisalat require you to have an Emirates ID to be able to take out a full-year sim plan and only offer tourism packages that are most of the time capped on how many minutes and how much data you get.

The best provider, in my opinion, would be to go direct to Virgin.

They allow you to take out a year package without initially needing your emirates ID.

They also offer 50% off when you pay for the plan outright, for the year, which will save you a load of money and you don't have to worry about monthly bills.

It's essential in the real estate world to make sure you have enough minutes and data because the job is constantly on the go.

THE VISA PROCESS

Getting a VISA in Dubai can be a long process but luckily for most, it is done by the company that employs you as they will be your sponsor.

Before you move, it's best to have a passport picture ready as you'll need it for a few different documents.

When you arrive in Dubai you will be stamped in the country via a tourist visa in your passport. This gives you 30 days in the country without paying or needing any paperwork to be in the emirate.

Visitors and tourists can apply for the second renewal before the expiry of the first one against AED 600 for each time of renewal.

Visa overstayers who do not renew, as above, will have to pay AED 100 fine for each day of their overstay, to be calculated 10 days after the visa expiry.

The process will start immediately and you will be required to do a medical test which includes a blood test and chest X-ray. Around 48 hours later, your passport will be stamped and your Emirates ID will then be in process.

You'll head for your biometrics to be done and then you will be given a physical ID card.

This then will allow you to open a bank account, rent a place and register for a car.

SIGNING UP FOR A BANK

Now you have your Emirates ID, you'll need to choose which bank you'd like to be with.

There are a few options and different benefits for each when you sign up:

Emirates NBD

FAB Bank

Abu Dhabi Commercial Bank (ADCB)

Dubai Islamic Bank

Mashreq Bank

Most banks with Emirates NBD but the choice is up to you.

You will need a salary certificate from your employer, your passport and your emirates ID. Once you have all the necessary paperwork, you can either head into the bank branch or contact the number below to come to your work and get you signed up.
Jatin Aror +971 56 841 3954

Your bank card and chequebook will take around 1/2 weeks to be delivered and once they arrive you can set up your online banking. I would also then transfer your money from your UK account into your UAE account. You can do this via a company called GC partners. If you contact the number below, they will talk you through the process, they offer amazing and low rates for moving your money across.

GC Partners +971 50 423 7586

Please quote "how to move to Dubai- Off The Bux" for the best quotes.

HOW TO GET A CAR

When working in a real estate role as a broker, you will need a car. You'll need to be able to get from one place to another for viewings and unfortunately, even though taxis are cheap, they will end up costing you more in the long run.

Before getting to Dubai, the fastest and easiest way to be allowed to drive in the UAE is to already have your license in the UK. That means that when you start driving in Dubai and have your Emirates ID, you will be able to change over your license and drive legally on the roads.

However, you can still drive without having your Emirates ID. As long as your visa and ID are in process, you are safe to hire a car although, you will have to use a private lease company to do so.

On the next page is a list of contacts that can get you up and running.

Then once you have all the documents you can then rent your car through well known companies, such as:

Carasti

Invygo

Diamond Lease

EZhire

My recommendation is to make sure you have your license

before moving. Driving tests in Dubai are much more lengthy and more expensive.

Car Contacts:

Al Emad Rent A Car - +971 52 413 6205

Amex Car 2 - +971 56 567 1085

Better Car Rental - +971 4 258 6331

Car Dealer Dubai Cheapest - +971 50 855 1334

Ayman hassan Car Rental - +971 55 558 7276

Car Rental Cheaaap Abbi - +971 50 741 0669

Car Rental Dubai One Click - +971 50 500 5886

Fadi Car Rental - +971 56 564 5656

John Calder Car Rental Dubai 4 - +971 55 558 7176

Manu Car Rental Dubai Check 5 - +971 52 242 4079

Moosa Car Rental Car Cheap 3 - +971 55 160 5858

Rent Car Dubai - +971 50 272 4243

Yoko Car Renta- +971 52 885 6397

I would recommend getting a few different quotes to see who can give you the best deal.

PLACES TO GO OUT

When you first arrive in Dubai, you'll want to go exploring the nightlife, the gorgeous restaurants, sandy beaches and pool parties.

As much as I advise trying to save as much money as possible and getting stuck in your job, you also need to give yourself a break now and again and turn off work mode because working too much can also be detrimental to progress. You will also be living in Dubai, which when you think about it, is crazy. So, take some time to explore what it has to offer and you'll also meet some amazing people on the way.

When I first arrived in Dubai, I worked 6 days a week and took one day off on the weekend to really wind down and enjoy what Dubai has to offer.

Top places to go and things to do:

Barasti - free entry for pool and beach and great way to socialise with other newbies in Dubai.

Marina walk - take a nice stroll around the marina or pick up a careem bike and cycle round for only 20AED.

Pier 7 - Great place to go after work for a few drinks and socialise with a few work colleagues.

Kite beach - public beach that has loads of fun activities, from jet skis to volleyball and loads more.

Top Golf - Gorgeous views and something to do that doesn't necessarily involve drinking, well you can if you want it too.

Boat parties - this is where you'll meet so many different people and potential friends.

Brunch - As we all know Dubai is very famous for its daytime brunches with unlimited food and drink.

I will list a few below:

Pool brunches:

Zero Gravity

Soul Street JVC

Wayne By Somnia

San beach

Aura Skypool

Drift

Cove beach

Twiggy

Ula

Dressy brunches:

Seven Sisters

Saffron brunch (Atlantis hotel)

Maidan Shanghai

Pizza express

Ce la Vi

Hell's Kitchen

Koyo

Asia Asia

The London Project

Coya

Zuma

Dubai offers so many good discounts for ladies' days so keep an eye out on social media such as Tik Tok to take advantage of this.

UNTIL NEXT TIME

I hope this has helped in some way or another and has given you an insight into how to comfortably make the move to Dubai with all the knowledge you need.

Make sure to be following my Instagram and TikTok accounts @x_elisestan to keep up to date with what I get up to on a day to day in Dubai and my messages are always open if you want to get in touch for any more advice.

Thank you for reading our eBook! We hope you enjoyed it and found it useful. If you would like to learn more about our work and keep up with our latest updates, please visit our website at https://offthebux.com/ On our website, you will find additional resources, how to get started with recommended products, as well as information about our team and how to get in touch with us.

We look forward to connecting with you and continuing the conversation.
Thank you again for your support.

Printed in Great Britain
by Amazon

22488877R00020